ABOVE: *A selection of jet beads showing the variety of design.*
COVER: *A faceted collarette type necklace and a fine shell cameo in a twisted ribbon mount.*

JET JEWELLERY AND ORNAMENTS

Helen Muller

Shire Publications Ltd

CONTENTS

Set in 9 point Times Roman and printed in Great Britain by City Print (Milton Keynes) Ltd, 16 Denbigh Hall, Bletchley, Bucks.

Small jet articles for the desk. The taper holder is mounted on an ammonite. The paper knife was made for Miss Polly Rhodes in 1880 and has her name on it.

A crescentic necklace of jet beads found in a bronze-age burial at Portalloch, Argyll, Scotland. Note the typical dotted decoration on the spacer plates.

INTRODUCTION

Jet has been used as a jewel and talisman for over four thousand years. The ancient Greeks and Romans called it *gagates* and in the first century AD Pliny wrote in his *Natural History:*

'Gagates is a stone, so called from Gages, the name of a town and river in Lycia. It is black, smooth, light and porous and differs but little from wood in appearance. The fumes of it, burnt, keep serpents at a distance and dispel hysterical affections: they detect a tendency also to epilepsy and act as a test of virginity. A decoction of this stone in wine is curative of toothache; and

in combination with wax it is good for scrofula.'

Since Pliny's time we have improved our knowledge of its chemical and physical properties and learnt to take its medicinal properties with a pinch of salt!

Jet is a type of brown coal, a fossilised wood of an ancient tree similar to our present-day *Araucaria* or monkey puzzle tree. These trees flourished in the Jurassic period about 180 million years ago. When the trees died, they might fall into a swamp or river and eventually be swept down to the sea. On the way the tree would be

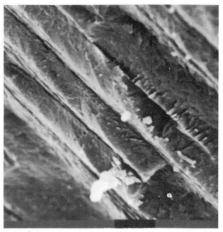

ABOVE: *An electron-photomicrograph of jet which shows the tube-like vessels of the original wood magnified about two thousand times.*

LEFT: *At the top is a typical piece of water-worn jet. The skin has been removed and the edges rounded by the action of the sea. At centre and below are two pieces of mined jet showing the yellowish or bluish skin and the typical conchoidal fracture.*

broken into trunk and branches and when these became waterlogged they sank, to lie for millions of years at the bottom of the sea. Dead and decaying organisms, mud and detritus, falling on top of the wood, caused great pressure, which flattened the branches and together with chemical changes altered the wood to jet. Analysis of the oil contained in hard jet has confirmed that it was formed under sea water, while it is probable that soft jet was formed in fresh water.

There is little difference in appearance between the so called hard and soft jet. In fact they both have the same hardness, but hard jet is tough and durable, while soft jet is brittle and tends to crack when worked or subjected to heat.

The nineteenth-century workers of Whitby were convinced that jet, like amber, was a solidified resin. Both were very light in weight and had the fascinating property of picking up bits of paper and straw as they developed static electricity when rubbed on wool or silk. It was for these reasons too that the Romans were unable to distinguish between the two gems and called jet 'black amber'. Studying a thin slice of jet under a microscope gives conclusive proof of its woody origin, for the annual rings of the original wood can often be seen. In exceptionally fine specimens of jet these annual rings can sometimes be seen with the naked eye.

Today we can study jet under an electron microscope and with its very high magnifications we can see the vessels of the original wood.

Chemically, jet is a carbonaceous material containing about twelve per cent of mineral oil and traces of aluminium, silica and sulphur. When jet is worked a brown powder is produced and if a piece of jet is rubbed on unglazed porcelain it gives

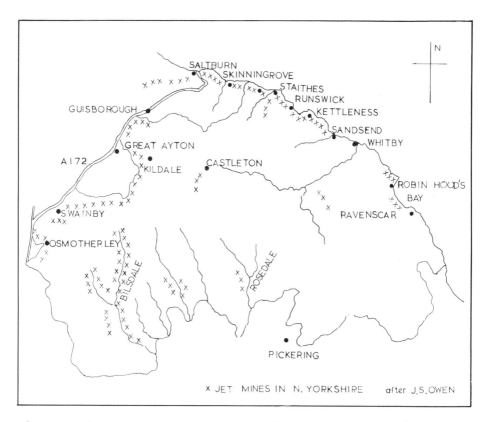

X JET MINES IN N. YORKSHIRE   after J.S. OWEN

a brown streak.

Jet is very light in weight (specific gravity 1.3) and has a hardness of 3-4 on Mohs' scale. It breaks with a conchoidal (shell-like) fracture and burns with a smell of burning coal. Jet takes such a high polish that it can be used as a mirror. It is a poor conductor of heat and so feels warm to the touch. The colour of jet is unique; its blackness is so intense that the expression 'as black as jet' has been part of our language since the twelfth century.

GEOLOGY AND MINING

Jet is found throughout the world, although not all of it is hard jet. Very little is known scientifically about the differences between hard and soft jet or between jet, lignite and cannel coal. Therefore we can say that a type of jet is found in Russia, Turkey, Germany, France, Spain, Portugal and North America as well as in England.

Works of art from Germany and Spain show that hard jet was found in these two countries. However, there is no doubt in the minds of Yorkshiremen that the best hard jet of all comes from around Whitby.

In North Yorkshire jet is found in the Jet Rock Series, which occurs in the Upper Liassic deposits at the base of the Jurassic rocks. This series of rocks is approximately 95 feet (29 m) thick, of which only a layer of 25 feet (7.6 m) is the jet rock proper. The best hard jet is found in the upper 10 feet (3 m) of this layer.

Two landmarks helped to guide the jet miners to the jet-bearing rock. First, the jet rock contains a species of ammonite called *Harpoceras exeratum* which is quite distinct from other fossil molluscs found in the surrounding shales. These ammonites were often incorporated into jet jewellery and ornaments.

Secondly, the layer immediately above

5

Inside an old jet mine. The miner worked into the hillside until he came to a 'face', where the shale was too hard to work. Then he retreated, pulling down the roof behind him. In this way he worked up to the Top Jet Dogger and found much of his best jet. The jet rock pulled down from the roof raised the floor of the drift so that it is only possible to crawl along it now. The old mines are very dangerous and since they are completely worked out there is nothing to be gained by venturing inside.

ABOVE: *The spoil heaps from old jet mines on Carleton Bank near Great Ayton. The path once used by the miners is now part of the well known Lyke Wake walk. Driving along the A172 from Osmotherley to Stokesley on a fine day and looking to the right, a row of these old spoil heaps can be seen following the contours of the hills.*

BELOW: *The shale on the spoil heaps weathers out into thin sheets, each one representing a year's fall of sediment. The shale is grey in colour. Sometimes shale heaps would ignite spontaneously and burn for many days, and afterwards they appear a salmon pink colour.*

the jet rock is a band of limestone called the Top Jet Dogger. This weathers out into large discs known locally as 'mermaid's dining tables'. The Top Jet Dogger also provided a strong roof to the adits which were dug below it into the jet-bearing shale.

Soft jet is found in the bituminous shales above the jet rock and in rocks of the Middle Jurassic.

The Upper Lias outcrops in the cliffs around the coast from Ravenscar to Whitby and then again from Sandsend to Skinningrove. At Whitby the jet rock dips under the sea to form the dangerous Whitby rock. Some of the jet rock occurs in very inaccessible areas and the easiest to reach are those north of Whitby, particularly in the Runswick and Kettleness area.

Jet occurs sporadically in the jet rock, being found in thin seams or nodules. In some places where rich deposits were found the workers excavated tunnels into the cliffs.

In the early days jet was found washed up on the shore or as a result of cliff falls after a storm. As the industry grew, this beachcombing could not meet demands and other methods of obtaining jet developed. One of these was *dessing*, whereby a man was lowered by a rope over the top of the cliff in order to reach the jet. This was dangerous and often proved fatal. Finally the miners turned inland, where they found that the jet was easier to remove from the surrounding shale, which had weathered over the years. They simply dug a tunnel or drift into the hillside using a long pointed pick and a shovel. The tunnel was just high enough for the miner to stand and work in. If it turned out to be productive the tunnel was continued right and left into the hillside so that eventually the land was undermined as though by a huge rabbit warren. In addition to this unsightly spoil heaps were formed of useless shale that was tipped down the hillside and as a result the miners were very unpopular with farmers and landowners.

Jet mining began in about 1840 and stopped around 1920. In the heyday of the jet industry in the 1870s about two or three hundred men were employed. Today jet is still found washed up on the shores and once again provides sufficient raw material for the few people who still work with jet.

A stone-age carving (above) of an insect larva 1½ inches (38 mm) long, regarded as a delicacy by the reindeer hunters who lived in southern Germany about 10,000 BC. A photograph (below) of a modern fly larva (Oedemagena tarandi) shows the similarity of detail. Today these larvae are still found under the skin of reindeer and are eaten by the inland Eskimos of north Alaska. Prehistoric men would wear these small carvings as amulets to bring success in hunting. Other finds in this area included a small jet hedgehog and a stylised figure of a woman which would have been worn as a fertility charm.

These two Roman pendants, from the third or fourth century, were found in Cologne and are similar to some excavated in York. They both represent the head of Medusa with the wings and snake hair and would be worn as a protection from the evil eye. Size 2¼ inches (57 mm).

THE HISTORY OF JET

PREHISTORIC JET

Jet was one of the first gems to be discovered by man. Ever since the stone age it has been made into small objects for personal adornment. To primitive men its electrical properties would endow it with magical powers and they would wear it as a potent talisman.

Some of the earliest jet artefacts have been found in Germany. Dating from about 10,000 BC, small amulets shaped as animals have been discovered in stone-age settlements in south Germany and Switzerland. One of these is shown on page 8.

From a neolithic dolmen in Couriac in France came a necklace of alternate jet and chalk beads. Jet was often combined in this way with bones, teeth, amber or other natural objects.

In Yorkshire the earliest jet jewellery is found in bronze-age barrows. Beautiful necklaces consisting of rows of barrel-shaped beads with rectangular spacer plates have been found in many such locations, not only in Yorkshire but in Derbyshire and as far north as Scotland. One of the finest examples is illustrated on page 3. Not only were three such necklaces found in Derbyshire but also two sites have been found where bronze-age man worked the jet. From the half-finished pieces discovered at these sites it is possible to deduce the methods used by these primitive people, 4500 years ago, to produce such a variety of jet jewellery. The jet was probably shaped using slabs of sandstone. Continuous use will wear a groove in the stone and a piece of jet rubbed over it will naturally acquire the barrel shape seen in so many of the old beads. The jet could be drilled using a tiny chip of flint and a simple bow drill and finally polished with its own dust mixed with oil. In this simple yet skilled way necklaces, rings, bracelets, earrings, pendants, toggles, V-perforated buttons and belt sliders were made.

Not all the artefacts which were supposedly made of jet were made of hard jet. Some were made of soft jet, cannel coal, lignite or Kimmeridge shale. Archaeologists of the nineteenth century who excavated these old barrows were unable to distinguish between true jet and these other natural substances and therefore described them all as 'jet'. Examination of many will reveal that much of the soft jet and lignite have disintegrated but the hard jet retains its polish and after four thousands years looks as though it had been made yesterday.

ROMAN JET

It was from the Roman name *gagates* that the German *Gagat,* the old French *jaiet* and the old English *geat* were derived.

When the Romans invaded Britain they were very impressed by the high quality of the hard jet which they found in North Yorkshire. By the third century AD they were producing rings, bracelets, necklaces, pendants, dagger handles and dice as well as diestaffs and hairpins. Excavations of Roman sites all over Britain have unearthed these artefacts, the most interesting of which came from Eburacum (York). When excavating the foundations of the old railway station there, a whole jet workshop was discovered containing tools and half-worked pieces as well as articles of jewellery. The raw jet came from the Whitby area and the finished pieces included a number of pendants in the form of Gorgon's heads. These were identical in design to pendants found in Roman sites in the Rhineland of Germany, particularly in Cologne.

In the Roman and Germanic museum in Cologne can be seen large numbers of jet artefacts including dagger handles, small carvings of lions and bears and all types of jewellery. These pieces are identical in design and execution to those found in York. Since no jet workshop or half-finished articles have ever been found in Germany it has been concluded that they were probably manufactured in York and exported to Germany. The authorities are in no doubt that the jet is from Whitby. After the Romans left Britain the use of jet for jewellery declined.

MEDIEVAL JET

In the seventh century AD Christianity came to Yorkshire and for the next thousand years or so jet was mainly used for ecclesiastical jewellery. Rosaries, rings and crosses were made for the monks of Whitby Abbey but very few items survive from this period. In Whitby Museum can be seen a jet cross which dates from the fourteenth century and was found on a witch post in a cottage at Egton. The magical qualities of jet allied to the symbolism of the cross would be a very potent protection against evil. It was widely believed too that jet was a protection against dogs and so it was worn by poachers!

In Europe also jet was mainly used for religious objects. In France the industry, which was centred on Sainte-Colombe in the department of Aude, specialised in very fine rosaries.

From the fourteenth century to the sixteenth there was a flourishing jet trade in Schwäbisch Gmünd in south Germany. It was in this region that stone-age jet objects were found as well as a large amount of Celtic jet jewellery from the iron age. By the fifteenth century the jet workers were organised into guilds. Jet turners and jet carvers had separate guilds and neither was allowed to do the work of the other.

The objects made here were mainly of a religious nature–crosses, statues and particularly rosaries–and it was perhaps because of this that during the Reformation the German jet trade declined, to be replaced by the silver and gold trade, which still exists today in Schwäbisch Gmünd.

In Spain jet is found in the provinces of Asturias, Galicia and Aragón. The Spanish word for jet is *azabache,* which comes from the Moorish word *cebecha* meaning a black stone. The Moors wore a jet *higa* or phallic hand to protect them from the evil eye and this practice continues in Spain today.

From the ninth century AD jet was used to make souvenirs for the pilgrims to the shrine of St James at Santiago de Compostella. The badge of the pilgrim was the pecten shell, symbolising eternity. These badges, together with rosaries, crosses and statues of St James, were made in the workshops in the *Azabacheria* or Place of Jet near the Cathedral. From the thirteenth century there was a thriving jet trade, the workers being organised into guilds called the Brotherhood of Jet Workers.

Like the German trade it declined in the seventeenth century but a small amount of jet is still being worked. In the *Azabacheria* today there are two workshops and about ten shops selling jet jewellery and souvenirs to tourists.

ABOVE LEFT: *This beautiful pieta, made in 1530, is in the museum at Schwäbisch Gmünd in south Germany. The jet is obviously of high quality. Height 3½ inches (89 mm).*

ABOVE RIGHT: *A Roman jet pendant or betrothal medallion (third to fourth century) depicting a man and woman in relief. At the top is the loop through which a thong was passed for wearing around the neck. After all this time the jet is in excellent condition. This and other jet artefacts can be seen at the Yorkshire Museum, York. Size 2 inches (50 mm) across.*

RIGHT: *A sixteenth-century statuette of St James. In his hat is a pecten shell, in his right hand a staff and in his left hand the Bible. Many of these statues, varying from 4 to 7 inches (100-180 mm) high can still be seen in museums today. In some of them St James is accompanied by kneeling pilgrims and on the base may be written 'Ora pro nobis, beate Gacobe'.*

LEFT: *A necklace made in 1760. The beads are crudely carved and flattened in shape. The incised patterns are of shamrocks, roses, leeks and thistles. Each bead is drilled twice and double threaded. Size of bead 1¼ inches (32 mm).*

BELOW LEFT: *An elegant widow c 1880. Not only is she wearing jet jewellery but her dress is also decorated with jet.*

BELOW RIGHT: *A lady in a crinoline wearing a long jet chain, earrings, a brooch and two bracelets, c 1860.*

Mid Victorian brooches were large to suit the full dresses. Acorns and oak leaves were popular motifs. The oak tree was the mythical abode of the thunder god and the acorn was considered a charm against lightning. The ivory carving is probably Swiss in origin.

THE WHITBY JET INDUSTRY

From the time the Romans left Britain until the beginning of the nineteenth century there was no organised jet industry as there was in Germany and Spain. References in the literature show that jet was well known throughout the period and there is mention of jet workers in Elizabethan times.

In the eighteenth century a few local people were making crude beads and crosses using only knives and files. It has often been written that the introduction of the lathe in 1800 was the reason for the start of the Whitby jet industry. This did give a better product and at a faster rate than the old method. However, the success of an industry depends as much upon

selling its goods as it does on producing them. Jet sold for a variety of reasons which all came together in Victorian England.

First, there was the growth of the railways, which brought people from the newly industrialised midlands to the coast for that novelty, the seaside holiday. Wherever they went, the Victorians liked to take home a souvenir and naturally from Whitby it was a piece of jet.

As the century progressed, fashions changed from the lightweight clothes of the Regency period to the heavier and darker dresses which culminated in the voluminous crinoline of the 1850s and 1860s. As always, fashion in jewellery followed and the fuller dresses required much larger jewellery to compliment them. For this jet was ideal, for very large pieces could be worn without the discomfort of extra weight. The jewellery from this period is very bold and bulky.

After jet was exhibited at the Great Exhibition of 1851 it attracted attention from the continent and in 1854 Isaac Greenbury, a prominent manufacturer, received an order from the Queen of Bavaria for a chain 6 feet 4 inches (1930 mm) long and another from the Empress of France for two bracelets. The royal patronage was very important. Already in 1850 Thomas Andrews was advertising as 'jet ornament manufacturer to HM the Queen'. When Prince Albert died in 1861 Queen Victoria entered into a long period of severe mourning, during which time only jet jewellery was allowed to be worn at court. The people followed court fashion and the etiquette of Victorian mourning became so strict that with the high infant mortality of the time some women wore black for most of their married lives. This did not mean that they wished to be dowdy or unfashionable. On the contrary, they were very elegant and wore a great deal of jewellery.

So the Whitby jet industry grew from two shops employing twenty-five people in 1832 to two hundred shops employing fifteen hundred men, women and children in 1872. In this year a good craftsman could earn between £3 and £4 a week (a great deal of money for the time), and the annual turnover of the industry as a whole was said to be £100,000.

Jet workers were to be found all over the town, in large purpose-built shops, such as that of Charles Bryan, who employed 120 men, in tenements and attics or even in small wooden lean-tos, where one man lived a hermit-like existence, eating, sleeping and turning out beautiful jet jewellery.

Jet worker Mr J. W. Barker in his workshop, chopping out jet with a chisel.

Mr Barker hand carving. On the bench in front of him are the chopping-out block and a lathe. Attached to the bench are strips of emery cloth for rubbing down the grooves and hollows in the design.

THE MANUFACTURE OF JET JEWELLERY AND ORNAMENTS

The miners sold their jet to the rough jet merchant, from whom the manufacturer bought his supplies. At the start of the working day the foreman of the shop handed out the jet pieces to the workers. Each piece was carefully studied for size, thickness and quality in order to decide what it was to be used for. The best pieces were reserved for the skilled craftsmen who carved the statues, cameos and other prized articles. The very thin pieces could be used for monograms, while the cheapest jet, often imported from Spain, was used for beads.

Rough jet, when mined, had a skin or *spar* of a bluish-brown colour, from the shale in which it was found.

First, the skin was removed, using a heavy chisel of iron or steel with a handle weighted with lead. All the movement was done with the wrist and no mallet was used. The jet was then ready for *chopping out* into pieces of suitable size and shape. This was done either with the chisel, against a stout piece of wood attached to the front of the workbench, or with a disc saw fitted to the lathe. It was very important that the minimum of waste occurred at this stage. Small cut-offs could be used for beads.

The chopped-out pieces were then ground on a 14-inch (355 mm) sandstone grit wheel, which took off the rough corners. The jet was wetted and held against the side of the wheel. It was then passed to the craftsman who would complete it by cutting, carving, engraving, inlaying or any of the specialised arts required for that particular ornament.

If it was to be carved, the worker would use his own simple handmade tools, which might have been made from an old file or piece of hacksaw blade, with a handle of leather wrapped around an old clothes peg or cartridge case. They looked very crude but they were treasured, sometimes being handed down from father to son. With these rough implements the craftsman could fashion the most delicate designs, sometimes with a sketch in front of him, often with the design only in his head.

The first process was *leading*, polishing on a lead wheel to remove the scores and grinding marks of the sandstone wheel and, in the case of a brooch for example, to give a flat base. The piece was held against the flat side of the lead wheel, which was also homemade. They melted some lead in an old frying pan with a little antimony and tin around a central wooden stake. When cold, the lead was mounted on a lathe and, while turning at speed, was shaped with a cold chisel until it was about ¾ inch (19 mm) thick, tapering to a knife edge.

The leading was done wet with the aid of a little *rotten stone*, a fine abrasive river mud of a creamy white colour, which came from Derbyshire. The rotten stone was contained in an old tin tray under the wheel and a splashguard, which might be made of an old trouser leg, hung over the front of the wheel. All cutting was done on the edge of the lead wheel and an intricate diamond-cut pattern could be done in a few minutes.

When the piece required drilling, a lathe was used, fitted with an old umbrella spoke; this seemed to be more successful than a conventional drill bit. The articles were usually carved first and then drilled, a delicate operation, because if the piece cracked much time and effort had been wasted.

The final process was polishing on a succession of wheels which they called *boards*. Only the first of these, the *pig's bristle brush*, was called a brush. The *listing board*, which came next, was also homemade. It consisted of 1-inch (25 mm) strips of wool, usually cut from old woollen garments, wound tightly around a wooden core. With both these boards rotten stone and water were used to give the first polish; then the article had to be carefully washed to remove all traces of rotten stone and dried in a box of sawdust.

The final high polish was given on a series of boards of walrus hide, porpoise hide or leather, or using a *rouge wheel*, a soft brush of pure hair. With these boards they used a mixture of jeweller's rouge and oil called *copperas*, which gave the workers, as well as the article, a reddish hue, earning them the nickname of Red

Some of the jet worker's tools: a lathe with a lead wheel attached and in front, from left to right, two drilling chucks, a small pig's bristle brush, four small lead wheels, a disc saw and three hand carving tools.

A rather large and ornate necklace from the mid Victorian period. The necklaces were often secured by ribbons threaded through the end pieces so that the length of the necklace could be adjusted to suit the dress. The matching brooch should also have two rings pendant which have been lost.

Demons! It was replaced later by a mixture of lampblack, paraffin and linseed oil, which brought out the deep black velvety lustre of the jet. A final polish on a *shag board,* a wheel of chamois leather with shaggy edges, and the craftsman's work was done.

Now the women took over, threading the beads on a beading board, affixing the backs to brooches, mounting on cards and pricing. The hooks and fasteners all came from Birmingham and were nearly always of base metal. Gold and silver were seldom used except as decoration.

THE DECLINE OF THE INDUSTRY

During the peak years of the industry the supply of hard Whitby jet was not sufficient to meet demands. So local soft jet and soft jet imported from France and Spain were used, mainly for beads, which can easily be recognised today because they are always cracked. Since this happened soon after the beads were made it gave the industry a bad reputation.

The workers in Whitby were convinced

A page from Joe Lyth's pattern book and on it two of his hand tools, a design ruler and three bar brooches made by him. Mr Lyth's workshop is now preserved in the Castle Museum, York.

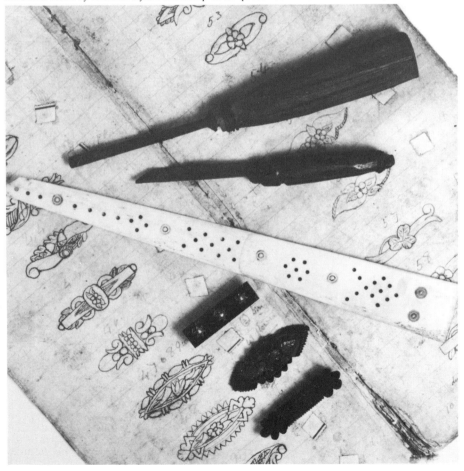

Mr J, W. Barker in his workshop with his apprentice, Joe Lyth. Mr Barker was the last man to be indentured into the jet trade and his indenture can still be seen in Whitby Museum. Mr Lyth was the last man to be apprenticed into the trade and served a full seven years apprenticeship under Mr Barker. Here they are leading. Notice the large wooden flywheels, 2 feet 6 inches (760 mm) in diameter and 4 inches (100 mm) thick, worked by a treadle, Leather straps connect the flywheel to a pulley on the driven shaft. Under the lead wheel is the box of rotten stone and on the wall are naked gas jets.

that this was the cause of the decline in the trade and in 1890 they attempted to introduce a trade mark and guarantee of the quality of jet.

Alas, this was only one of the reasons why jet was losing favour. In 1887, when Queen Victoria celebrated her Golden Jubilee, she finally agreed to relax her strict mourning and the British people turned with relief to lighter and gayer colours. The crinoline went out of fashion and the new dresses had a much smoother line.

Unfortunately the jet craftsmen of Whitby could not or would not change with the times and the large dark jewellery did not suit the fashions of the Naughty Nineties. They also had to compete with imitations. Cheap mass-produced plastic copies were flooding the market, vastly undercutting the more expensive hand-carved jet.

By 1884 the number of workmen had dropped to three hundred. Worse was to come: at the turn of the century Art Nouveau, with its delicate pastel shades and flowing lines, had no place for black. By 1921 there were forty men working in the trade. Now Art Deco was the rage and one might have expected jet to come into its own again for black and white was the prevalent theme. Onyx was used universally in Art Deco jewellery. One wonders why jet was not used for these eminently suitable geometric designs. Jet jewellery of that period is found with paste stones but the designs are still Victorian.

By 1936 only five craftsmen were left, making souvenirs such as eggtimers, penholders and other small items for sale to tourists. In 1958 the last trained craftsman died and with him the art of the Victorian jet carver.

ABOVE: *Tokens of affection. The locket at the top would be worn by a young lady and carried the photograph of her betrothed. The locket at the bottom of the picture could be worn by a lady on a ribbon or by a gentleman on his watch chain. It would have her hair on one side and his on the other. Notice how plain the inside of the locket is. Top left is an unusual combination of a vulcanite heart on a jet base. The brooch in the centre of the picture shows the popular use of paste stones in the 1920s.*

TOP RIGHT: *William Wright's retail shop in Whitby in 1890. The workshop is behind the mirrored door on the right. The glass-topped counter is preserved in Whitby Museum.*

BOTTOM RIGHT: *This old man with his portable jet shop was a well known figure; he stood at the bottom of the church steps in Whitby.*

Jewellery with religious motifs. A beautifully carved cross with the initials IHS, a hair locket with the initials IMO and a locket with the initials AEI. Jet lockets can be distinguished from vulcanite copies because the jet under the glass compartment is left rough and unpolished, whereas the insides of vulcanite lockets are moulded in an attractive design.

Some of the more talented craftsmen specialised in carving heads of the well known personalities of the period. These two cameos were made by William Stonehouse about 1870. Left is the Emperor Francis Joseph of Austria, 1830-1916, and right, Charles Dickens, 1812-70.

Only a small proportion of jet jewellery was mourning jewellery. None of the colourful pieces on this plate could have been worn in mourning. From left to right, top, a hand-painted Italian porcelain miniature and a pietra dura or Florentine mosaic. Bottom left, jet combined with ivory and, right, a pink shell cameo. In the centre a fine shell cameo in a cleverly carved jet frame. The shell cameos were imported from Italy and the classical heads were copied in jet but in a higher relief. It is said that cameo carvers from Naples came to Whitby to teach their art to the jet carvers.

LEFT: *Bar brooches were very popular from the mid Victorian period until the 1930s. These show a variety of techniques—diamond cutting, inlaying with mother of pearl, and small pearls in gold stars. The brooch next to the bottom contains a polished ammonite. At the top are two name brooches. Since many of the Victorian jet workers were illiterate a large wall placard of names was hung in the workshop from which they copied the letters, not always successfully as the second brooch shows.*

BELOW LEFT: *This brooch was sold as a souvenir in Scarborough in 1899 and depicts a typical army camp of the period.*
BELOW RIGHT: *A pair of cameo earrings by E. H. Greenbury, a well known artist of the 1870s who won many prizes. Victorian earrings always had hooks: there were no studs or screw fittings until the twentieth century.*

RIGHT: *This photograph, c. 1880, shows how the Victorian lady carried her watch on a jet chain. The chain was secured at the neckline by a jet brooch and then hung down below the waist and into a little pocket at the waist where the watch was kept.*

BELOW LEFT: *A selection of jet bracelets, all on elastic. Solid bangles were made in three sections and joined by glue and wire but they are now very rare. This type is most commonly found today.*

BELOW RIGHT *This bust of Mary, Queen of Scots, is an example of the very finest workmanship.*

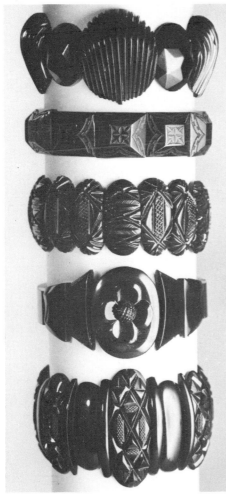

*Typical designs in vulcanite. The hand holding a wreath, a basket or a rose is a very common design.
Although presumably copied from an original design in jet, the author knows of no example of a jet
hand of this type. The rather intricate and beautiful motifs decorating the lockets are all moulded and
applied to the surface: designs in jet lockets are incorporated into the case. The beading around the
cross and the pendant is characteristic of vulcanite work as is the shape of the pendant. Again, the
cameo face is applied to the surface of the pendant, whereas jet cameos are in one piece.*

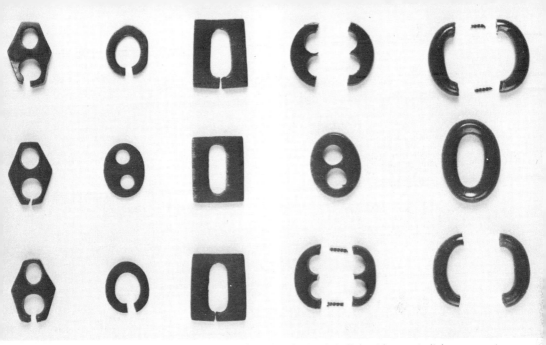

Left, the construction of vulcanite chain links and, right, jet chain links. Alternate jet links are sawn in half and then pinned and glued together using ockamatutt, a mixture of shellac and Collins glue. Vulcanite is thermoplastic so the links can be opened and joined together.

IMITATIONS OF JET

Imitations of jet include cannel coal, bog-oak and the man-made vulcanite, Bakelite and black glass (French jet). These last three were made in large quantities deliberately to imitate Whitby jet. Hence they are still found today being sold, albeit unwittingly, as jet.

The process of hardening rubber by treating it with sulphur was invented in 1846 by Goodyear, who made tyres. Sometimes called ebonite, *vulcanite* was black when new and took a good polish but when exposed to sunlight it faded to a khaki colour. Like jet, vulcanite gives a brown streak on porcelain and a brown powder when scratched. The only conclusive test is a hot needle, which in jet produces a smell of burning coal and on vulcanite gives the unmistakable smell of burning rubber. Since most antique dealers do not look with favour on customers who stick burning needles into their jewellery, how is the collector to recognise vulcanite?

The important point to remember is that while all jet jewellery is hand-carved, vulcanite and all plastics are moulded. With a lens it is quite easy to see signs of moulding, rounded edges, raised stippling and sometimes an intricacy of design which could not have been achieved with a hand tool on jet.

Vulcanite jewellery was mass-produced and judging by the repetition still found a hundred years later any particular design must have been turned out in thousands. Some of these are shown on page 26 and it is possible with experience to recognise these patterns.

Bakelite was not invented until 1909 so it was not used as extensively as vulcanite but many beads were produced and the plain round ones can be deceiving. Bakelite gives a black streak and black powder on scratching. Luckily many Bakelite brooches and bracelets are stamped 'patent'. The final test, as usual, is a hot

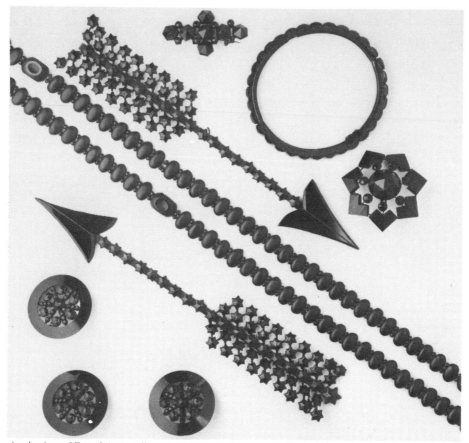

A selection of French jet jewellery, including a pair of arrows for the hat or the hair.

needle, applied in an inconspicuous spot, which in this case gives a smell of phenol (carbolic acid).

Epoxy resin imitations are being sold now by museums but are not meant to deceive. They are moulded and the back of the piece is often concave.

Although France had deposits of jet there was not enough to meet the demands of fashion in the nineteenth century. The French therefore produced a black glass known as *French jet*, which was mass-produced and very cheap. In England too black glass imitations were made but were called *Vauxhall glass*. It has a slight reddish tinge when viewed at certain angles to the light.

One of the great advantages of French

jet was that it could be made into very tiny beads which were used for dress trimmings.

There is no difficulty in identifying French jet. Glass is cold to the touch, heavier and harder than jet. It cannot be scratched with a pin and a hot needle has no effect.

Cannel coal is not usually made into jewellery but into ornaments and carvings. It does not have the deep black colour of jet but has a rather silvery sheen and does not take such a high polish. It gives a black streak and a black powder when scratched.

Bog oak is a fossilised wood found in Ireland and was never meant to imitate jet but it became popular in the nineteenth century on the wave of the fashion for jet. It is dark brown, still shows a woody structure and does not take a high polish. It is durable, easily carved and decorated with Irish motifs, shamrocks, castles and harps being the most common. The beads are usually decorated with a ring and dot pattern. Bog oak can be easily distinguished by sight and testing is not necessary.

Bog oak jewellery and ornaments. These are still being made today.

The work of three modern jet workers. The sea horse, the modern earrings (left) and the eye pendant made of amber, ivory and jet are the work of Alec Mackenzie. The reproductions of Victorian earrings (top right) are by Bob Coates and the ammonite and scorpion (bottom right) are by Gwen Tidy.

Miniature tables and chairs were very popular souvenirs. The men who specialised in this craft were known as 'furniture men'. The articles were often decorated with engravings of Whitby Abbey. Size of table top 2½ inches (64 mm) across.

MODERN JET AND HINTS FOR COLLECTORS

After being neglected for many years, jet is at last regaining popularity. We no longer believe in its magical powers but its beauty as a jewel is once again appreciated.

At least ten people are now making modern jet jewellery. Alec Mackenzie has a full-time job but spends all his leisure hours making a wide variety of striking jewellery by combining jet with ivory and amber. Gwen Tidy, a busy mother of three children, likes to combine jet with colours and experiments with paints made from natural pigments such as malachite. Bob Coates has taken over his garage as a workshop and can hardly meet the demand for his earrings and pendants. He also likes to repair and reproduce the old Victorian jewellery.

Amateur lapidaries find jet a rewarding material to work with since no elaborate equipment is necessary. A sharp knife, some files and emery paper and a lot of patience are all that is needed.

At the same time the antique jewellery is eagerly sought both by collectors and by those who like to wear it. It is still possible to buy these examples of nineteenth-century craftsmanship at prices far below those of other gemstones. Bar brooches are cheap but fascinating to collect, there being such a large variety of design. Naturally, the more detailed the workmanship, the better the piece. Since they were all hand-made it is seldom that two identical articles are found.

When collecting, the first step is to distinguish jet from its imitations. The condition of the piece is the next important point to look for and a lens is useful to detect cracks or repairs. A collector should try to find articles which have their original fittings, and beads should not be re-threaded. Victorian brooch pins were very large, often extending over the edge of the brooch, and never had a safety clasp. The only acceptable alteration to the original is the rethreading of bracelets, since the elastic is often perished and can be replaced with hat elastic.

It is a good sign if a piece is dirty for this usually means that it has not been restored. Jet can safely be washed in detergent and warm water, given a gentle scrub with a soft nailbrush and carefully patted dry. If the surface is worn, the polish can be restored by rubbing with some Brasso on a soft cloth and then washing. The glue from sticky labels can be removed with eau de Cologne.

Finally, jet should be kept separate from other jewellery as it is soft and easily scratched.

Collecting jet is made more interesting when the jewellery (below) can be compared with a contemporary portrait.

ACKNOWLEDGEMENTS

The author wishes to thank the following for their help and information: Mrs A. Kildale-Robinson, Mrs P. Clegg, Mrs B. Lyth, Mrs Kelly, Miss B. Todd, T. Roe, J. S. Owen, P. G. Hill, P. Pinder, L. Horne, E. Daniels, K. Birkby, G. Dürr, H. G. Muller, and Miss Katy Muller for typing the manuscript.

Illustrations are acknowledged as follows: I. Aisbitt, page 6; K. Birkby, page 4 (right); Kosmos Verlag, Stuttgart, page 8; Mrs B. Lyth, pages 14,15,19; H. G. Muller, page 7 (both); National Museum of Antiquities of Scotland, pages 3,11 (bottom); J. S. Owen, page 5; Römisch-Germanisches Museum, Cologne, page 9; Stadtisches Museum Schwäbisch Gmünd im Prediger, page 11 (top right); *Whitby Gazette,* inside front cover; Whitby Literary and Philosophical Society, page 21 (top); Yorkshire Museum, page 11 (top left). All other photographs were taken by Simon Pentellow of the photographic section of the Leeds University Audio Visual Services.